THE NAKED WELSH POET

****

Poetry & Rambles

From

The

Gower Coastline

Book Me A Read

Published online by Book Me A Read

ISBN: 9781520472553

Table of Contents

Book & Cover

Muscle vest pulling a muscle dog

Hard bristles on a desperate chin

Steel eyes looking with steal fingers

Brisk boots that rip up a concrete path

Harder than his dog can imagine

Falling apart at the seam the essence of real mean

The local menace is streets ahead of that old Denis

Look if you dare but stop before you stare

Folk stay clear under fear they quietly sneer

For this clown with a frown will bring them all
down

He is hard as nails if you listen to the tales

So his path remains clear as his steps draw near

'What's your name' asked a young lad without
shame

A rock face cracked as the jaw became slack

A long drawn silence met a small innocent defiance

'Tarquin' came the grunt from the mean looking
front

'That's a nice name' replied the boy in the frame

'Why do you look so mean' he asked looking keen

A long tense stare from the man with no hair

'No one talks to me, I'm so sad and lonely'

This stunned the young lad who thought, this is mad

'I'll be your friend, if it will help you mend'

His hard icy stare fell and left him bare

From scary and mean came a tear and a beam

'No one has been as kind as you' said the

menace that once belonged in a zoo

With friendly beguile the young lad did smile

This fearsome bruiser stood no more the looser

How a roll of the dice can bring something nice

BAG FOR LIFE

'Bag for Life' that's the question I get asked at every super market or shop counter. It seems like a reasonable proposition although very sinister and macabre. But in the context of what is being offered, it's a very good deal as long as it's not my life in question.

I've not taken up the offer as yet; I'm a little worried of the legal implications on purchase and how the unprovoked and fatal act is carried out.

If I accept the offer of 'a bag for life', I pay my 5p, as you do, then what happens?

Once the transaction is complete, will the cashier or shop assistant immediately leap into murderous action and take the life of the person who is next in queue? Or are there designated loyal employees willing to sacrifice their lives in exchange for the sale of a reusable plastic bag? Or worse is it my life that is taken once I hand over the 5 valuable pennies?

Is the life taken using the 'tag removal' gadget they have at the checkout? Will the person who loses their life have their head removed in the same emotionless manner used when removing tags from expensive spirits and razors?

I do wonder if there is an assistant store manager waiting in the wings with a Samurai sword or a Magnum 45. Once the transaction is complete he appears cool as a reduced price cucumber and says "Do you REALLY have less than 10 items in the '10 items or less' till? . . . . Are you feeling lucky punk? . . . . Guess you're not, you've just agreed to accept a Bag for Life . . . . . Asta la Pizza baby" does he then decapitate you with the razor sharp sword or fill your bargain hunting body full of life taking lead

Maybe we have the option to choose the life that is exchanged for the cheap plastic hold all. That 5p purchase is elevated when we are given the power to choose to emulate the grim reaper. Temptation would be to ask for two bags, double the impact. The worry is if the deep and dark side of the brain took over would the temptation be to buy £3 worth of bags, a bag for life would turn in to a massacre on a grand scale.

Maybe I'm looking at this in the wrong light, maybe the term 'bag for life' means to create life. Maybe the price of 5p and the purchase of a plastic bag will enable the buyer to do the necessary actions to create a life?

This again has its concerns, is the act of creating life completed with the cashier? The person behind you in the queue? Or again can we select an employee or a random person from the great British public?

If it is a member of staff that is going to help promote the 'bag for life' scheme how will this impact on their family life or relationship status? Surly this would need to be agreed during the recruitment stage of the person joining the retail outlet.

If we could select from the great British public I'm guessing there are going to be some mighty long queues behind some people, but sadly some are going to be left wanting and lonely.

This selection process will cause an imbalance to the structure of Britain; a two tier system will develop. We will see a two class status, those who have the physical assets that invite others to want to create life, and those who have the physical assets to repel life.

Legally this has issues; 5p for a plastic bag could give you at least 18 years of cost, worse if the child is a brainy bugger as the cost could carry through until they are 21 or more with university or other means of education.

This gives us the conclusion that a bag for life is probably aimed at the ending rather than creating of life, as cost will always prevail in the modern world.

Maybe I'll just carry or juggle my food and goods back to the car. The thought of a bag for life is a little too complicated for me.

The Bay

Quietly falling into nowhere
Hazy history is left in its trail
Warm hand of life caresses the beautiful bay
A blushed beach welcomes a cool breeze

Methodically climbing over and over
A white warrior churns up a golden land
Glistening silver particles dance over the clear swell
Heavy feet retreat from a day at the beach

PURE AND SIMPLE

Fall to my knees surrounded by trees
Birds they flutter with a tune they mutter
Filling their tummy some worms from their mummy
Leaves welcome a breeze, they chatter with ease
Light through the branches, this world it enhances

A few stray bluebells interrupt buttercup dells
The field so mellow sways to yield yet so feral
Bees are bobbing for pollination there is no stopping
Honey in the making the sweet prize for our taking
Nature at work with no time to shirk

There are nuts a plenty for squirrels so healthy
Foraging and collecting their food needs protecting
There's a long winter ahead they'll ensure their well fed
A red fox that wanders its prey stops and ponders
All lay low from this troublesome foe

Back on my feet miles from my street
No hustle or bustle I stand so quiet and subtle
I breathe in the air this tranquillity so rare
This world that surrenders me caresses and sets me free
With this beauty so rife I easily yield to this idyllic life

DRUGGED

Just one hit
Light headed and dizzy you float with the clouds
Your heart is beating out of control
These feelings and emotions are like nothing before
You're hooked

Easily under its control
Every minute of the day it's in your thoughts
It lingers on your lips, as everyone needs to know
Intensity takes a grip as friends are forgotten
You want more

It fills your veins and poisons your mind
Paranoia takes hold and weakens your spirit
Everyone wants what you have
Losing it isn't an option
Watching is not a choice
Arguments intensify and destroy

Hitting out is always never going to happen again
Crying has replaced laughter
Loneliness beckons as the end nears
Another life ruined

A month or maybe years of pain
Your heart and mind will work hard to recover
'Never again' is a convincing line
Whisper and remind yourself
'Love is a drug'

Special

It seemed a long wait to get to that date

It was all about June it would never be too soon

At last the day came my life never the same

With my very first look my heart you took

In my arms you came Kira would be your name

With the love that I had I was now your dad

Life was never slow as I watched you grow

From your beautiful young life you grew to be a wife

You've your own family to care time is so rare

Although our distance gets longer my love gets stronger

So proud and so glad that I am your dad

Flea fly and foe numb

A quick squirt and the job is done

Hairy bed and furry coat

All not spared in murderous rout

Brisk in step with glint in eye

A mite free moggy feels just the jobby

A gleaming coat and dangerous smiles

All set up for a night on the tiles

Humpty Dumpty sat on a wall

Humpty Dumpty had a great fall

All the kings' horses and all the kings' men

Couldn't put Humpty together again

How times have moved on. There is no way Health & Safety would allow an egg to sit on a wall. In this nanny state where we live, government policy would have legislation or an act banning the 'sitting on walls' or 'climbing of walls' by all shell-like characters. The wheeling and dodgy dealing Haggle Market of Parliament would not sanction wild and crazy 'eggs of today' getting over familiar with dangerous walls.

Even the oldest and most exclusive elderly care home in Britain, the House of Lords. Oh dear no! How could any of them support the flippant and arrogant eggs in their quest to flaunt and parade on the common wall? And if the good ol legal institution that holds this country apart fails to stop this dangerous wall sitting act, you can be sure the timid and cotton wool wrapping eurocrats would insist on banning adrenaline junked up eggs from having fun.

If a dare devil, hell-raising rebel of an egg were to go near a wall the authorities would 'throw the book' at him. Maybe not physically straight at him, maybe curve it a little and just miss the crazy shell-like dare devil. Or, if the book throwing was direct at the young smooth and shiny chick magnet, the book would need to be made of feathers not to risk the direct hit causing a fatal injury. When the egg steps out of line his shiny arse will be fried by the authorities.

But let's say a rebel egg stuck two yokes up to the system and bureaucrats. Let's say that egg climbed that brick wall and sat on the top in denial flaunting itself in the midday sun, poaching for all to see. But suddenly, without warning this brazen eggs life suddenly became in danger. Its shiny arse slipped away from the top of the wall. Humpty the adrenaline junkie Dumpty fell. Not just any ol fall. He had a great fall.

Humpty was now in bits at the base of the wall, scrambled for all to see. In all honesty do we believe that all of the kings or queens horses and men would rush to the aide of this young foolish base jumping shell cracking junkie?

More than likely the first person on the scene of this tragic accident would be a sales rep from a legal company looking to establish blame to aide a claim. Within seconds the form would be filled in with Humpty's runny yellow signature on the documents. The owner of the wall would then be set on by a frenzied team of wannabe solicitors looking for commission to feed on.

As for the kings/queens horses and men, they are all in foreign lands risking their lives for the safety and security of others in troubled countries. Or so the government says, although some would say that these good people risk their lives for the possible wealth hidden in these countries. If there were any soldiers present after this pitiful accident, we should question their role and ask should they be attempting major shell surgery on a young broken egg? Or are they eggspected to fulfil the duty of unscrambling the mess left by the wayward young yokes of today and their carefree attitude to rules and regulations.

How times have changed. There are Humpty's everywhere all waiting to crack, all waiting to become a victim of a tragic accident. Behind every accident is legislation waiting to be implemented. Waiting to prevent the loss of young eggs and the unnecessary spilling of yokes.

The debate will rage on for years as adrenaline eggs look to have fun and authorities will look to put them all in one basket.

The Tube

Vacant faces pack a metal tube

Metronomic beat keeps the heart rate steady

Rucksacks and bags claim territorial seats

An uneasy calm slows this human race down

A distant stop starts a frantic rush

Queuing at a door while the tube keeps moving

Being first is essential in this miserable race

No whistle or flag just a button in place

The beat picks up as the tube starts moving

Face phones continue their cold journey home

I Watch

I watch you grow

I watch you stumble

I watch you fall

I watch you talk

I watch you cry

I watch you laugh

I watch you go

I watch you return

I watch you develop

I watch you bloom

I watch you celebrate

I watch you high

I watch you Low

I watch you leave

I don't watch you anymore!

all of me and my toes

I can touch my toes
I can see my feet
When I feel the heat
I want to dance in the street

My eyes look to meet
My arms open to greet
I have a life tired and beat
Please don't retreat

My heart is open
But my soul is unspoken
Look a little deeper
You'll see that it's broken

Tell me about you
But not the whys and who
Say that your heart is not blue
Assure me that you're being true

Let's meet again
We can start as friends
My life is yours to spend
Please help my heart to mend

Goodbye remember to phone
Write to me when your home
My heart you can easily own
Just don't leave me all alone

I Walk

I first walk to my mother

I learn to walk to my father

I walk beside my sister

I walk to make friends

I walk from enemies

I walk from my home

I follow my heart

I follow paths given to me

I follow paths I find myself

I walk with sunshine before me

I walk with the sun on my back

I walk through heavy showers

I walk through low dark clouds

I walk with my head low

I walk into darkness

I walk no more

Night seers

Tall as the trees with no bendy knees

Straight into the air ready to share

Tall as the trees with no bendy knees

Straight into the air ready to share

Dull and grey with little to say

Dependable and loyal without a need for toil

They follow the dark then fade with the Lark

Wherever you may be they will be there to see

Orange and bright bringing aid to your sight

On every night the loyal streetlight

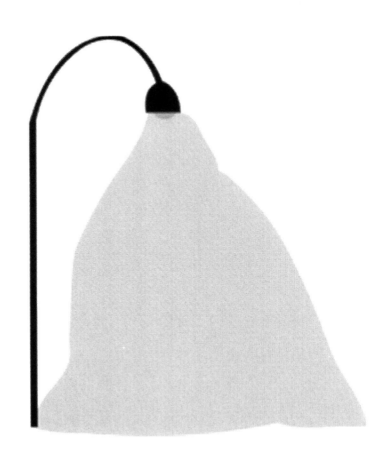

'Rubbish' is a brilliant example of random writing without a cause or meaning. Created by Nonny Hughes at the delicate age of 15 years during an exam she had no interest in. this piece rambles with amazing ease in and out of random topics that concerned a 15 year old girl during an exam.

Take yourself back to those teen exam years and enjoy......

I'm bored.

I've done all the swatting I'm going to do.

I don't think I can do any more.

This class is so quiet it's like a graveyard. Hold up! I hear some paper rustling and did I hear a cough then? I can't have. I think everyone's dead. Julia's writing like mad in front of me. I can't see her writing but I know she is because she's wiggling back and forth in her seat!

There is sign of life! Derek just got up to get some more paper. There's a swat! This bloke sitting opposite me looks stuck.

~~~~! That gave me a fight! The bell just went. I think I like Geraint a bit, (he just came in for the forms). I wonder how Louise is getting on. She's got a sort of graph in front of her now, it looks hard. We've got Mr Marshal overseeing us now. I wonder if he thinks I've got an exam, the way I'm writing here. I think he's looking at a rural science exam paper. I just saw a picture of a butterflie (I don't think you spell it like that do you?) Mr Marshal is giggling to himself. He just wrote something on the paper and now he's got a grin from year to year! (Ear to ear). I can see his bald patch!

Everybody is working hard. Simon just got some paper. Llinos looks stuck, she looks all red as if she's going to cry. Andrea just went out to get some paper and had a chat with Mr Muchallot (Mr Marshal). Julia just went out to get some paper. She says it's hard but she's got a grin from year to year (ear to ear. That's not funny anymore. Not that it was funny anyway!)

I'm watching Dafydd at the mo. That's why my writing is all up the spout! He looks bored and stuck. Come to think about it, everybody looks bored.

Mmm! They look nice! Oh! Sorry, just talking to myself there. Andrea's crisps I'm on about. Tomato or prawn I think they are.

~~~~! The bell. I wish it wouldn't keep doing that!
I've just decided that I like someone in this class. I'm not going to tell you that it's Ian just in case Mr Marshal catches me writing this and reads it out! The bloke next to me has finished his cem paper and Mr Marshal has told him there's an hour left. Mrs Marshal (Mrs Marshal??) well, he looks bored now too. It must be awfully boring being a teacher in this school. There's a jib. Mr Marshal looks as if he's in pain.

The boys are coughing one after the other now. Do you think it's some king of Morse code or what? I think someone is choking but I don't see what's funny in that. I'd better laugh, everyone else is.

I just caught (how do you spell 'catch' in the passed tense? How do you spell tense? As Eddie Tudorpole would say 'what is the meaning of life'?)

Enough of this lunacy! I just 'catched' Ian's eyes. He's stunningly cute but too short for me. But now, Dafydd, well, I mean.....!! What on earth is that he keeps his pencils in? It doesn't look much like a pencil case to me! He's stuck it to the desk with a drawing pin now. Oh well! He's cutting up his cem paper! Ian looks like a swat. Never mind he's still nice. Who cares if he's a swat? I like swats! (What are you on about girl?)

The bloke sitting next to me made a pattern our of paper and Mr Marshal just saw it. Per'aps it wasn't a rural science paper. I just saw a biol paper and it had the picture of a funny looking something on it, that I might have mistaken for a butterflee.

We've got 3/4 hour left.

Mr Marshal was just looking stupid at Iwan Jeffries because Iwan was nodding to him. I can't stand Derek. He gets on my nerves! He's probably cribbing like he would have done yesterday if it wasn't for Dafydd. Dafydd. Aah!

I just looked at him in the eyes and he smiles.

Thrills.

Mr Marshal is looking daggers as me. I think I've failed my commerce exam.

I've decided that there's an awfully odd shape on that mountain from where I'm sitting.

Julia looks sad. She's done a lot of writing. So far Louise hasn't been to get any paper.

I feel like vandalising something or screaming, but I'd better not.

Half an hour left. Great!

I wouldn't have minded knowing that Duncan bloke that Julia made friends with if he looked anything like Dafydd. The bell just went and all the boys as usual went Mmmmmmmmmmmmmmmmmmmmmmmmmmmmm (Oops! one m too many), with it.

Haah. He had to think about that one. A bloke just asked him how long he had left and Mr Marshall took five minutes to work out 25 minutes so really they've only got 20 minutes!

20 mins left!

Ian's smiling about something. He's not anymore, he's probably come to a hard question that even HE can't answer.

I can hear Andrea G shouting (well, not exactly shouting, more like whispering really) 'Rhiannon ow!' and now Rhiannon is showing her paper.

The bloke sitting next to me just pinched that fourth form boys stapler so that he could flick a staple at Darryl who is sitting in front of him.

He went to press the top and the staple just fell out onto the table. Not funny eh! Well it was when he did it! He just went to flick a bit of selotape at Darryl and that fell on the floor in front of him too (not in front of Darryl!)

There's a swat Julia is. She's still writing. She's probably written two books down on the paper already and now she's on the third! Louise is a swat too, and she's the one that said she didn't know anything. As if!
oooooo ooo ooo ooo
Happy, happy talking, happy talk

I absolutely despise that song. I hate it!

We've got 10 minutes left and I can't wait for the bell to go (to go where?)

10 mins left!

Simon just asked if he could borrow Ian's stapler and I think he asked the answer to something. Either that or they had a chat about something else.

I wonder what Alun (my Alun) is doing now. Not a lot I should think. He's probably out with his girlfriend but I don't mind, it's nothing to do with me.

We've got 5 minutes left. This is Grrreat!
I haven't done any swatting for welsh this morning, I've been writing this. I would fail my welsh anyway.

What this? 'Haven't a clue', 'clue', glue', oh! glue? Right, I get you, you want the glue. Oh! I'm so clever. 'Na', 'Da', Oh Ta, right, thank you! I'm great at this lip-reading stuff.

This bloke sitting next to me likes AC/DC. Goodness knows why mind. I hate them! Don't let Alun catch me saying that. Well, it's not up to him, is it ?
Louise has finished and Julia. Iwan just did something and Louise burst out laughing. She's got a mad laugh. You could hear her a mile away!

I'd better finish here because the time is up and I mustn't keep on writing after 'time' is called must I?
I've just got a last two words to say - I'm bored!

The end ☺

Shadow

I try to look at my shadow with integrity
I don't recognise the person I see
He is a fake, he is weak, he is not me
I don't want to see this person

How can I meet the person I hope to be
I see someone who exists beyond my own limitations
I see a person who is unlike anything I can be
I want to be that person so much

I despise who I am
I want and expect so much from me
I desperately need to be different
How can I be this person I see

How do I convince my shadow I am worthy of its presence
There is a height I cannot reach and a depth I see too often
I cannot kid myself, I cannot hide from reality
Learning to accept me is teaching me to accept failure

My life is too heavy to lift from these entrenched depths
Failure is something I carry with ease and disconcerting
comfort

My soul distances itself from this lost cause
I walk without presence in a life I failed to live

I cannot look at my shadow
I am alone feeling I have nothing inside
Emptiness fills my soul with pain
Hurting others can't stop me looking for a way out

My shadow beckons me towards the darkness that I no
longer fear
When light becomes a beacon with no answers I cannot fail
to avoid the question
So I will follow the path of my shadow
I will become the darkness I seek

MY little GIRL

Can I still hold on to my little girl as she blossoms into a
young woman?
When did she grow up, why did she have to grow, so soon,
so quickly
She has her own little girl growing; this is telling me that I
no longer have a little girl
Her look is reminding me that my thoughts are delusional,
unreal and out dated

When did I stop waiting for a star to fall with my little girl?
When did the hugs stop being so instinctive and become
awkward
When did I stop being the only man in her life?
When did someone take away from me the best job I've ever
had

Am I wrong, when I recognise my happiness turning into heartache?
Am I wrong to care and love someone so much?
Did I often say she would grow into a fine young woman?
Did I ever listen to what I often said?

Am I wrong to feel hatred and anger for someone who took my sunshine?
Am I right to show restraint and reason while my heart feels so much pain
Am I so proud to see her take on the hard relentless pressure of a difficult life?
Am I wrong to want to hold and shield her from this less than ideal life?

Do I feel guilt for being part time for so many precious years?
Will I ever stop missing the time lost to upheaval and selfishness?
Is it only me that felt missed through these spiteful years?
Was this the catalyst that took her away from being my little girl?

Will I ever forgive myself for not being a real dad, regular
and normal, just there?
Do I think it's time for this pain and heartache to go?
Do I deserve to reach a day when beating myself up becomes
an option or choice?
Will time ever cure this pain, will I ever have that much time

From my position at the base of her pedestal I look with
admiration and respect
I can see this very special young woman; I see her strength
and beauty
I can still see my little girl; I can still hold her now and then
I will always love my special little girl

Recipe for Life Cake

10 oz Sugar –
6 large eggs
4 oz mixed nuts
2 tonne self raising flour
Several measures of alcohol, of your choice
1 oz ginger

We start the recipe as we start the new year with a good splashing of alcohol, we separate the eggs only using the white of the eggs… these we whip to a frenzy, just like we do at the start of the new year.. we hype our expectations of the coming 12 months, believing that they will be better than the previous year.. as for the yellow part of the eggs we discard them like we do the previous 12 months.

Sweeten the new year, this acts as a balance to the bitter (ness) that life often brings. 2 tonne of self raising flour, still may not raise the quality of my life, whereas a dash or more of alcohol will mask the bitter taste of life an forget about this bloody cake. As for the mixed nuts, they always seem to find me, plague me and make my life hell.

As for the small amount of ginger, that's life !!

1. have a drink

2. measure 10 oz of sugar

3. have another drink

Drawn to a light

Far away from this fight

It's not the sun

It's not that bright

It's all I have

So I'll keep it in sight

'Shall I compare thee to a summers day'

The opening line from William Shakespeare's 'Sonnet 18'. A rather beautiful line that opens the sonnet and points the reader towards an idyllic summer setting and the flicker of love through the verse.

Or is it?

Heavens golden eye shines on a summer setting that is blessed with the darling buds of May and serenity.

I believe that William was blessed with a rarity in this summer free land. At this moment in time it would appear that Mother Nature wasn't up to her meddling and confusing tricks. William fell upon a real life genuine summer's day complete with bright yellow sun, warmth, flowers and tranquility.

Sadly it can be said that a summer's day is the last thing we see on a summer's day. The complex job of getting a bright yellow glow to appear in the sky during the summer, especially during the school summer holidays is almost impossible.

To compare thee to a summer's day in our time
would evoke a different kind of visual experience. I would
be comparing thee to torrential rain, gale force winds and
dark miserable skies. Would I be saying that the comparison
I offer is suggesting a grey and cloudy appearance, dowdy
personality supported by enormous disappointment and a
cold damp shiver?

I would possibly suggest that the comparison offers insult
not warmth or love. I would expect the recipient to compare
thy face with a punch bag and lay heavily into me with the
force of a thousand Tysons. It's not big, clever or romantic.

For the sake of replicating the nature of the sonnet, we can
pretend the summer's day is blessed with the eye of the
heavens and the sun is pouring its warm rays over a bud
blessed field. This is where the scenario takes another
awkward twist and opens up a weakness in the ideology of
the sonnet. Most of us Brits are not use to the sun being
present in the summer. We struggle when the golden rays
reach our slightly pale and overweight bodies.

So the image projected from the comparison sees us being compared to a large sweaty pink person feeling like shit as the sun flogs an unprepared pale body. There is an image of red burnt skin, soggy armpits, sweaty foreheads and mangy toenails poking through hardly used sandals. Coupled with this hot scary image is the constant swatting of flies and the crazed helicopter action needed to repel feared wasps and other flying foe.

Adding to this scary look is the need to be in a beer garden fuelled with 10 pints of ice flavoured cider. The sweaty soggy pink person turns into a slurring swaying saliva dripping demon. A need to hydrate using alcohol becomes a necessity as thousands gather to moan about the insane heat and the price of sun cream.

The aftermath of a real life summers day sees Boots increase profits; ice-cream sales boom and the sound of 'flip' and 'flop' carry throughout the land. After years of moaning about the rain we change our winge direction and slate the blistering heat that grinds us to a sweaty halt.

I feel this isn't the image William looked to project with his comparison. I believe he caught a glimpse of how a summer's day could be seen and enjoyed. This moment has lasted hundreds of years captured in words that sell beauty and love. Would William have had the same impact if he wrote his sonnet in a beer garden tanked on watered down cider, draped over a bench, wearing flip flops a baseball cap and with soggy armpits? Could we really grasp this loving comparison?

Thankfully we are able to share this beautiful sonnet as it was meant. Thy comparison will live on while we can breath and see and will continue to give life to thee.

CHILDREN'S BOOKS OF OLD

How many kids have been damaged by the so called
children's books that parents have force fed generations?
They seem innocent, yet tell tales of murder, deception and
acts of violence.

Take poor old defenseless Chicken Lickin! Poor innocent
sod that had a question with no answer. All he wanted to do
was learn. Initially you may feel this is a simple tale of
colonel Sanders, his 11 spices and an unhealthy addiction to
chicken, but it's not!

It's a children's tale of deception and murder. This poor little
chicken and some other poultry set off to ask a serious and
understated question, 'why has the sky fallen'? Instead of
answers only media tycoon Murdock could answer, he gets
tricked into going back to a foxes den for food! That ol
chestnut. Unknown to the young Lickin, this 'back to mine
for food' is used by foxes all over the world and the poor
little yellow pecker didn't have a hope. He took the cunning
ol hairy scavengers word thinking he was a decent kind of

creature. With simplistic trickery and deception the innocent bird was taken back to the old foxes den. How often is this replicated on a week end in a city center near you?

Once back at the foxes humble abode, the small yellow defenseless Lickin was brutally attacked and murdered. He was then eaten as a mini fillet with fries and a Pepsi. The fox even used a smelly lemon wet wipe from a little sachet to clean his chops n fingers.

Was the fox very cunning? Or was chicken Lickin just too trusting and basically thick as shit for falling for 'that ole trick'?

Where was his interfamily training, lessons and values that should have been handed down through generations of

Lickin's? Where were his parents? Where was his 'safe guarding' adult or at least someone with Parental Responsibility to advise and care for this stupid bird?

These days it's all too easy to blame someone else. We are all aware that sly ol foxes are out in our communities, ripping the life and young blood from them, taking all the good Lickin's from society.

Why aren't we doing more as responsible adults to warn defenseless birds of the greedy old animals that pray on the young, stupid and innocent?

Look at that young and innocent Red riding in da hood. This young person was not cared for by an appropriate adult, being allowed to wonder in a dark wooded area is very dangerous. Surely there was a child protection issue here?

Where were her family, neighbors, friends, and were the hell were social services when you want them? They were too bloody busy trying to get a teenager to attend school. This delicate young girl had the emotional impact of a wolf hounding and harassing her through the dark and dangerous woods. She was then confronted by the same wolf after he had swallowed her grandma whole!

The emotional and psychological impact on the young person is no doubt far more than she should have experience. With all this emotional impact, she then bravely confronted the wolf as he displayed unbalanced sexual signs of cross dressing and challenged him regarding his table manners and his unprovoked munch of her grandma.

Her bravery was nearly rewarded with an untimely death of nearly being eaten by this cross dressing wolf but luckily she was saved by an axe wielding killer. She watched this strange and aggressive man with an axe attack the wolf, cut him in half, and open him up. She then watched her frightened grandma who was naked (as the wolf had taken her clothes), walk out of his bloody belly alive! True to form and typecast shortly after her ordeal she made a pot of bloody tea! OMG! Did the crazy axe man or little red hood herself not think of calling the emergency services or at least NHS Direct?

Thankfully this incident ended positively for the little red riding hood. It could have ended in tragedy for the girl.

Again we ask where were the Police, Social Services, her parents, family members, anyone with decency and a moral obligation to safeguard and protect young children and gullible birds?

It is safe to conclude that Children's books of years gone by have helped mould those who are troubled today. Those loose cannons and slightly unhinged individuals were the innocent kids that sat quietly in bed while a vicious nasty parent read such evil books to them with a callous smile on their face.

I believe it is not the fault of the child and to a degree not the fault of the parent. Responsibility must take its place at the foot of evil writers of children's books.

"As Dull as a Brush"

'You're as dull as a brush'

How often have you heard someone say this or have you been told this by someone? Or have you used it to judge some poor soul who has just demonstrated stupidity on a grand scale or said something that has confirmed that person to be the dullest person you've ever met?

Yet another age old saying that has been abusively handed down through generations as children hear those immortal words that will carry them through school and beyond. The same words they will learn to offload to their own children in a cycle of put downs that will help sweep away the confidence of the young.

But what of its origin and behind the scenes meaning, what was this saying before it became famous. This ramble will try and dig the dirt on these seemingly innocuous few words. I will bare my own theory to its existence and meaning.

For the record and legal purposes
'I state that it is my belief that not all brushes are dull. Any comparison to brushes is a genuine fluke, there are no named brushes or intended malice or malicious comments intended to any bristle head out there with insecurity issues'

The insult is comparing the recipient to that of a brush, a dull brush to be precise. So the giver of such an insult believes that brushes are dull, stupid and brainless. Or if they are bright bristly brushes then the original spat was probably given by a person far more intelligent than the brushes known to him or in his company at the time. With this being an insult, I believe that the person giving it was not at the top of the class in school. Someone who would know personally how dull some brushes can really be. So my guess is that it would be someone who frequents with bristle heads on a regular basis.

So to establish the first part of my theory, a really stupid person who happened to know some really stupid brushes is likely to have coined the insult.

The second part of my theory looks at why so many brushes are deemed dull.

There are many millions of brushes worldwide. Many different sized poles, many different colours, and many sized heads with different degrees of hair ranging from a full 80's perm to a baldy brush with a bristly comb over. Brushes are an integral part of society and manufacturing. They first gained public notoriety many years ago making cameo appearances in the cartoon Tom & Jerry. After a period out of the limelight and a few depressions they became heroes during the second world war helping to sweep away debris from bomb beaten battle scared cities.

Their status as heroes descended to that of lazy co- workers of council employees, building site labourers and road maintenance trainees. The one time Great British bristle head had now become a prop for the lazy and work shy of this once great nation. Britain gathered dust as the work force stood still and embraced unionism and an early finish. This is evidence in how the brush lost its purpose in life and became a symbol of laziness. It failed to see the damage that was being impacted on it from those it propped up. A brighter brush may have seen the light and detached itself from the work shy.

The third part of my theory reiterates part two and confirms another lost chance to establish itself in society.

There was a time when hope appeared in the shape of a pan. Not all was lost and despite the poor reputation the brush was establishing for itself, it could have been so different.

Pan burst on to the scene in a big way, it made the country sit up and watch and work. It gave brush a life line and joined up with the bristle head to create a double act only bettered by Morecombe and Wise.

Dust Pan and Brush was on everyone's lips. It seemed they were destined to be in every home across this great country and the world over. Sadly, soon after starting this infamous double act and relationship, cracks slowly began to appear. They developed a bitter rivalry, hatred spewed over into the tabloids as each tried to out do the other in a vicious and unscrupulous 'kiss and tell' that was to sweep the nation.

Households throughout the county wept as the split became evident. No more would they make light and clean up in all the right venues. They were now detached. Pan would be seen propping up bars while brush would be hanging about with cars and windows everywhere. Soon brush's relentless partying left him drained and washed out. During this period of shameless sweeping about in dodgy hotels with everyone and everything, JML had brought out brand new slinky gadgets that would sweep the nation off its feet and leave the brush out in the cold.

I reiterate the third part of my theory behind brushes demise and highlight how dull it was not to capitalize on its relationship with Pan. This was significant as after the world could see that pan and brush would never stay together, the chance of world domination passed. Pan went on to form a different double act with Teller; they wowed the world with magic and trickery.

My fourth part to this theory looks at the 'dull' part of the insult and further reasons why we see brush as being dull.

Now we now that dull is meant to describe grey and dreary weather, food that is bland, a goalless draw between two defensive Italian football sides or the live coverage of question time at the Houses of Parliament. We also know that dull is a true reflection of those with few brain cells or the ability to use them. There are some who went through school in the lower section of the banded grading. These were affectionately known as the 'clay class' collective or the 'tin bangers' these were the poor souls who were generally labelled 'dull'.

So what has the brush done to get the label of 'dull'?
It would seem that back in the day the brush alone with Elbow Grease had a nice little earner going on. They both worked hard during the week. Once paid the Elbow got to move freely in the pub, throwing copious amounts of beer down its throat.

Brush didn't pick up on this. It didn't pick up the opportunity to at least claim half the spoils or to a lesser degree get in on some of the drinking action. Despite Elbow often being on the minimum wage, Brush still failed to capitalize on a good little earner for its hard work.

Used and abused and not part of any of the Unions, Brush became over worked and never paid. Elbows all over the world moved on to bigger and brighter lives. Some using machines, shovels or keyboards. Sadly Brush remained at the bottom of the social structure.

Again this theory is pushed forward with evidence highlighting how dull a brush is.

This ramble has highlighted how stupid dull is. It has evidenced how the brush and dull have worked hand in hand over the years. We all know what dull is, we have seen dull, sat next to dull, and some of us are dull. Are we as dull as a brush though? That is something you will only know you're not by being clever enough to know someone who is. If you are dull as a brush you will normally dispute the accusation, and often punch the deliverer of this bold and sweeping statement.

We can clearly see why the insult uses the Brush as a marker to the degree of dullness someone can be. We can accept that if someone is as dull as a brush then they passed levels 'thick' and 'stupid' many moons ago.

But next time you see a brush, think not only once about this bristly bone head that is more likely to be dull, but think twice and offer some empathy for the wooden wonder with the dusty history. For that bristle baring battle scared hero helps keep this country clean.

Heavy Days

It all gets too heavy day after day

Carrying a pain that's too hard to say

The heart becomes laboured and the head starts to fray

I ask the question 'Is it worth the stay'

Ending this life is a price I easily pay

Come Back

I look into your eyes see deep, I can see why you
look to weep

All the troubles that you store are locked behind the
cold steal door

Your barriers surround you high, never an answer
when asked why

The hurt that you protect with might has left you
meek yet still with fight

Open up and let me near, I'll protect you from what
you fear

Trust me to ease your past and help bring a smile to
last

Your eyes once dark with tear now sparkle where
they use to fear

Let my heart warm and comfort thee and bring back
the woman and your love for me

Counting pinkies toe to toe
All correct and present don't you know

From left to right they all stand tight
Dirty toe nails, oh what a sight

They wiggle and jiggle on a cold tiled floor
Time ticks away behind a white locked door

Another recount passes the time away
The fluff between them destined to stay

White and shiny the room is tiny
Queuing outside those waiting get whiny

A tiny little squeak and the mist start's to reek
One large leak and the belly goes weak

A clench and a wrench and the pond gets darker
With a few more putts to see becomes harder

A tug at the roll will cleanse the soul
But with one sheet left your now way out of your
depth!

She doesn't know

Watching ......waiting, looking and longing
nervous and not noticed
Pink puffed cheeks guard the sweetest of smiles
A passing stare at her long blonde hair
Retreat into the dark and drift into the distance

Another day unnoticed, waiting and watching
Her smile to others sets a spell to enchantment
Eyes that eclipse the brightest sun
From dark and cold shadows I watch
Hope kept alive by the warmth of a love unknown

I move closer, I can see her lips so tender
Her soft smooth skin so close I can almost touch
I look away quickly, I look to the skies
She doesn't know who I am
Will she ever feel the love I have to offer?

Every day I see her beauty so pure
Every day I long for the warmth of someone so special
Should I share with her my wishes and desires
I still watch from a distance
My courage to pursue such beauty drowned in my own
disbelief

I will still watch my love from a distance
A shadow behind her curtains, two tables away in a café
I am the cold shiver in her dark shadow
She will never know…

Rather Than

Rather than build them up, we pull them down

Rather than see them shine, we let them tarnish

Rather see their back, than front up to their existence

Rather shrink in self-pity than stand in acceptance

Rather embrace denial than take on the truth

Rather be hostage to expectancy than be free to challenge reality

Rather maintain deceit than change to challenge redemption

Rather lash out at weakness than live amongst reason

Rather take on hate than look for tolerance

Rather accept easy lies than look at difficult honesty

Rather whisper in corners than announce with conviction

Rather berate and ridicule, than offer encouragement

Rather provoke anger than negotiate peace

Rather blame others than accept ourselves

Rather cast judgment than look beyond difference

Rather hit out at someone than beat up yourself

Rather take abuse than search for respect

Rather live in others shadow than exist in our own life

Rather you show me honesty, than arm me with distrust

Rather you show me who you really are, than allow me to
know someone else

Rather live with exaggerated self-belief, than exist on
rationed self-doubt

Will you stand by your inner truths, or hide behind
convenient barriers?

I want you
I can see you, I want to hold you
You are very still, inviting yet unaware of my needs
Without care and with ease you seduce me

I want you
That uncomfortable feeling trickles through me
I try to look away
But each minute my thoughts are with you
My need for you grows

I want you
I move around the room avoiding you
Everywhere I go you are with me
There is no avoiding you, I can't be without you

I want you
My life is always complete when I'm with you
I can't get enough of what you do for me
You penetrate my soul and ease my mind

I want you
I've let my wife and family go for the need I have for you
You are in my thoughts when I wake
It's you I'm with when I fall asleep

I want you
There is only you left in my life
I have no desire no will or want of anything else
My life is complete

I want you
Without you I am nothing
You are Drink, you are alcohol. I crave you and need you
You have my life

GUY FAWKS

Remember, remember the 5th of November!

Guido Faukes, or Guy Fawkes as he became commonly known, was born on April 13th 1570. He was staunch Catholic and passionate about his chosen religion. So much so he became a member of a group of Catholic conspirators who plotted and attempted to blow up King James and the Houses of Parliament. The story is well known in modern Britain, the young and passionate wannabe fire starter assembled copious amounts of gun powder below the House of Parliament. As the members assembled for the start of the winter session Guy lay waiting. With fuse and spark he aimed to open Parliament with a bang the likes the country had not seen. His aim was simple; blow up the building and kill King James and as many parliament members as possible.

My ramble consists of the following concerns. I am aware that as a country we are proud in our tradition of celebrating various events and historic occasions. We are passionate about recognising valour, courage, bravery, endeavour, life saving discoveries and good for nothing celebrities. Card and gift shops fuel the British want and need to keep traditions alive and kicking.

But on this well documented day, what are we actually celebrating?

We are really celebrating and recognising the efforts of a wannabe mass murderer. For many years the celebration was known a s 'Guy Fawkes night'. On these nights bonfires were built with effigies of Guy placed on top. Adults and children would assemble around the bonfire and watch it burn, happy to see the effigy of Guy burn with it. In the past, young wannabe 'Alan Sugars' would peddle these effigies looking to make money. 'Penny for the Guy' would echo around the streets in every town and city.

Currently in Britain we spend a small fortune on fire works or attend displays celebrating this wannabe mass murderer. Should we be doing this? Should we honour him on the day he tried to kill so many innocent-ish people? I use the word ish as these people were politicians. With that thought in mind, that is probably why he is celebrated. He tried to do what many of us want to do. In modern Britain how many of us wanted to blow up this 'old school' of educated layabouts who strip the country of money. High wages, deception, cash for questions, expenses, jobs for the boys and countless other underhanded ways to earn a more than decent crust. Where is our modern day Guy, who will carry the mantle he so innocently held.

I ask a simple question, if we are to continue to celebrate this wannabe mass murderer, should we celebrate other like minded souls who have pushed the dark depths of their mind and committed crimes that have scarred communities and history? Will we have a Hitler day? Or maybe a Ripper Day? Remember, remember the Ripper in November! Genghis days could be celebrated for all the wrong reasons, just as a Ted Bundy fun day could bring families together in a celebration of food, drink and all that is dark.

While I believe that these other names would not be celebrated in the way Guy is (unless Tesco or these Card companies get a whiff of a profit to be made) I do believe that celebrating someone who tried to kill so many people is rather wrong. I should encourage this barbaric night of multiple banging and whooping and wooowing to stop. But I feel if it is bringing families and communities together and encouraging people to smile while enjoying hotdogs and burgers, then who am I to grumble.

Christmas SHOPPING

Immediately after the fireworks fade, November sees the High Street brace itself ready for a frenzied attack from millions of frantic shoppers keen to part with their well-earned cash or benefits. It is that time of year again. The time of year that starts earlier and earlier every year.

The festive spirit is out spooked by the scary thought of crazy shoppers buying up everything and anything. Kids throughout the Land rub their hands with joy as parents are brainwashed from every angle. TV, Radio, Newspapers and High street shops throw countless adverts at the adults sponge like heads.

Aimless shoppers wander around and around, from shop to shop and although every shop will be different, it will be the same few Christmas songs that brainwash the unsuspecting shopper to freely open their purse or wallet and throw countless amounts of money at cashiers. This emotionless brainwash that would appear to be kid led ensures that shelves are emptied and Christmas trees are rammed up to the fairies frilly knickers with presents that are destined for that dark and smelly space under the bed.

There are many theories to how this crimbo collaboration works. The one I'm drawn to is that of the early and innocent visit to schools that parents pass by. It's around the start of the new school year when the mighty high street stores sponsor various events such as 'road safety', 'train awareness', 'get yourself illuminated and seen', 'healthy eating for school kids' and 'stranger danger part 2 sweets are not the only fruit'. It's at these child friendly events that the super duper high street stores get to mingle and interact freely with kiddies of all ages under these so called child friendly causes.

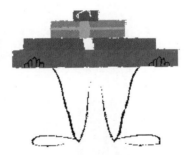

But secretly as they mingle and mangle behind the backs of unsuspecting parents, toy deals and alerts are being arranged. This high powered secret communication is setting the trend for a Christmas crime that befits the seasonal weather; cold, chilling and will freeze the life out of an innocent credit card. In a deal brokered similar to a Wall Street Hedged funded frenzy attack on equity-less properties, the latest toys and Britain's most wanted gadgets are agreed. After this, high street shops will aim a ruthless attack at parents and wallets. Sales pitches, radio and T.V adverts, banners and street criers all shout and push the 'most wanted list'. Crimbo songs etch into the hearts of innocent shoppers with the subliminal message 'spend, spend, spend'

That special day arrives. Charismas day as its known to children, repossession day as its known to parents. Over worked and over shopped parents watch as their little angels tear countless colored paper and shred thousands of ex trees to get at the 'surprise' that they never knew they were getting. Good ole Santa rides again, he and his helpers get 8% of the seasonal profits. This Christmas lark is a nice little earner and all under the slippery guise of good ole tradition, religion, pagan ritual and festive merriment.

TAKEN

Green glass eyes catching sun drenched light
Warm muzzy breeze tickling a quiet lost voice
Solitude for company while a waiting game is played
Sitting on a bed knowing never is too soon

Seconds take a beating heart into minutes and hours
A picture frame window captures a heartbroken sun
Soft tender hands press into a pale fragile body
While dark forced fingerprints are left to fade into dusk

A confused mind is focussed by the return of another night
Green fades to grey as eyes look towards fear
A cold shivering body halts a lonely isolated tea
Bruises are buried under a dark lonely night

A sorrowful moon hides behind a drifting grey cloud
Anticipating ears find a creaking stair
A Forgotten childhood hides behind a slow opening door
Crying eyes close on another violated night

Clear as Night

When birds have no song and the clouds have moved on

The night is so clear and the moon seems so near

When the stars look so bright and twinkle extra light

They say they hold the souls of our old

Of our lost and loved, our special ones above

They watch as we cry and miss them up high

Our lives are blessed when to them we confess

All our days that are bad and things that keep us sad

We miss them so much and the warmth of their touch

From the skies so high they can hear our sigh

Those stars shine bright and keep us in sight

They watch and protect, their warmth they project

They twinkle from above and fill us with love

10 to 1

10 pints tonight, he already wants to fight

9 minutes from home, his girlfriend's alone

8 texts sent to try, his happiness to buy

7 times this year his fists left a blur

6 days of remorse, 'never again' of course

5 visits to A&E, her 'accidental' fall is what they see

4 her own life she will fear every time he is near

3steps from the front door, she knows what's in store

2 night she will cry and pray not to die

1 punch away, with her life she will pay

Shhh . . . . It's Ok

Hush now conscience don't make a sound, don't listen to
your heart while angers around

Scream to your demons as they take your mind on a deep old
journey until dark you find

Block out the good and all that's bright, you can't spend
your life only living in light

Anger and rage its thirst you will quench, as your past is
released with its bitter stench

Your pain and hurt once more in the frame, as your head
reminds you life's not the same

As anger ebbs its tears you will cry and sit and wait for your
heart to sigh

Another free-fall into the black abyss, thinking of someone
you dearly miss

Only help

It's 2am under a clear dark night
I work alone till a new day and light
With pen in hand I look to write
I'll tell the world of my poor ol plight

With thoughts a plenty I sit and sigh
I ask the question, 'Oh bloody why'?
I get no answers although I try
I guess that's why all I do is cry

Just Those

With those I see I try to be me

With those I hear I try to bring near

With those I feel a friendship I steal

With those I pain my sorrow will remain

With those I miss to feel one more kiss

With those, you know who, my love will be true

Night Shift

Nearly sleeping but not quite awake

It's 4 in the morning for goodness sake

A snapping head shakes a dreary eye

A breath of fresh air under a clear night sky

I work at night and it just ain't funny

It's a cruel way to make some money!

A king's castle

Wandering this land until I could kick some sand

A gypsy stagger that found a dagger

Straight through my heart, at last a start

Out of my rut I found this Tin Hut

This king was crowned a castle I found

Night after night no need to fight

Basic and cold this place I behold

This peace is sound this comfort I found

At last I see the real me

No need to roam at last I'm home

I Need to Rest!

It's all too extreme with the best bits a dream

Both poles apart each playing with my heart

My eyes wide with delight my extreme world of
light

My extreme depth of pain head and heart a strain

The big void in the middle its reason no riddle

I travel with speed until desperate my need

After a few anxious sips the glass stays on my lips

Then I linger for a while there's no frown or smile

Just a hazy mess where my head can rest

MISSING BEAT

This heart stopped beating when you passed away
Before it restarted a single beat did stray

It's not been the same since you went and left
One day it will give up and lay to rest

No more pain and hurt for me
My soul set free for your eyes to see

I will then take back my missing beat
Only then will I finally feel complete

LOSING

I breathe in a new day

My eyes wide with anticipation

I see some light, its travelled far to be here

It warms me and holds me

My beaten heart reaches out

Hope forces just one more step

My head searches for a reason

A cold breath rests on my broken back

Darkness doesn't need to travel

It's always here

The touch from someone I'll never hold

The look from someone I'll never see

The warmth from someone I'll never feel

The love from someone that will never leave

My thoughts of someone that will never be
forgotten

forgotten

Close my eyes and I will still be seen

Block my ears and I will still be heard

Tie my hands and I can still be reached

Cover my mouth but my words will not be lost

When I stop thinking I will still be thought of

When my heart stops beating I will still be loved

After I am gone will I still be remembered?

Full Up

There's not much room in this old head

The frayed grey matter is feeling like lead

Some memories so bright I feel so happy

Others so dark and make me feel crappy

There are those I cherish I give them my love

Their warmth I feel like the sun from above

There are those who are gone I no longer see

I'd do anything I could to have them with me

There is sun and light when a new day breaks

There is darkness and pain as my old heart aches

It's You!

A few grey clouds and the rain start's falling
Another summer's day without the yellow beam calling

I look through the window and my mind starts to wander
Back to the day my heart grew fonder

You shone through my clouds your light from above
It was from that day I knew it was love

We walked through life and kicked up some sand
I'll go anywhere with you, you've my heart in your hand

2U

Mad I am to want you true
Crazy you to want me too

Our lives prepped and all but ready
Since we met we're going steady

Together we grow our lives ferment
At last in life we are both content

With a perfect view we turned a page
From that night on we were engaged

Soon is the day you'll be my wife
And so sweetly complete my life

I'll hold you tight and not let go
Because my heart loves you so

RPx

2U2

What if life didn't turn out to plan
The flowers the wedding and my 'perfect man'
What if his heart belonged to another
Life's tapestry would unravel, loves candle will smother

Would I curl up and die with my broken heart
Would I fight through the pain and make a new start
After years of lies, would it leave a mark
Impossible to distinguish the light from the dark

Then out of the dark, would I find a new friend
Someone caring and kind who'd help my heart mend
As the months would go by, the closer we'd get
Remembering the day that we'd first met

Years would pass by and stronger we'd be
Our lives stitched together in life's tapestry
He'd ask me to marry and I, with a smile
Would accept his offer to walk down the aisle

Now what if that 'broken plan' was the plan
I go through the hurt and find the right man
The one who'll be with me and never apart
The one I love with all of my heart

RPx

Just a Clown

No need to worry and no need to frown
Life's a bloody circus and you're the clown

Your emotions in a canon and feelings on a wire
All these bloody hits and you want to shout fire!

The audience always laughs and you stumble to the floor
You pick yourself up and prepare for some more

The circus keeps moving and the Ringmaster will sigh
Those tears are for real and every night you cry

Find me

Its dark, the room is dark,
I sit on a chair, alone in the dark
I can't see my life
I think it's gone

I sit quietly alone, the room is quiet
I can hear my heart beat slowly
I can't hear my life
I think it's gone

I reach out my hand, I reach out to touch something
I can't touch anything
I can't feel my life
I think it's gone

I try to speak, I want to talk about my life
I can't seem to say anything
I don't know what to say
I think it's gone

I try to scream, I want to shout loud at my life
I can't get my words out
I feel alone with my life
I think it's gone

I stand up, I want to walk away from my life
I don't know which direction to walk
I can't walk away
I think it's gone

I want to think, I need to think about my life
I don't know what to think anymore
I don't want to think anymore
I think it's gone

I want to hide, I try to hide from life
I don't know where to hide
I can't hide anymore
It still hasn't gone

I found a way, I can be free from my life
I know what to do now
My life is no more
It's finally gone

GONE forever

Taken from me and gone forever

Lost and alone in a different world

Clinging to pain as a constant reminder

Searching for memories amongst the congestion of hurt

Life goes on they all seem to say

This hurt will remain as a cancer through my veins

I'll not hold on to this pain forever

As forever will be here long after I've gone

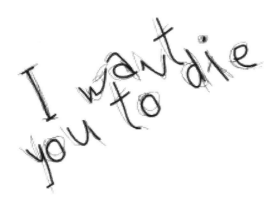

I want you to die
You will take my light and darken my soul
This pain is not for you
These arms that have held you close must let you leave

Your love has enriched my soul for so many years
My life has lived with meaning
Our hearts have always shared the same beat
I must continue this life alone

Your life was about giving and to others you gave light and
hope
It is not right you should feel pain that has no bounds
This cannot be for someone as special as you
My Love, you have to die

I will carry your heart with me always
The love you leave will share my life with the emptiness I
will feel
My memories will comfort me until our souls reunite
I will hurt my life over for the love I have for you
You must die before I do
Don't fear the dark your eyes can now see, the longest sleep
awaits you
Close your eyes, keep your thoughts close to your heart
Let love take you from me

Books and Downloads

From

Book Me A Read

Athena and the dream Catcher

Many years' earlier Wales had been cursed by the evil Dream Catcher.

He had once been promised the pure thoughts and dreams of ten Welsh children. These dreams would lighten his gloomy, dreary world and make his sad life sparkle again.

In return he pledged to give Wales hills and mountains, rivers and lakes, cliffs and beaches; in fact all the natural beauty that you can still see here today.

The deal was signed by the Elders of Wales on a golden tablet hewn from the mines of the north.

And the Dream Catcher made good his promise.

Using all his powers with spells and wizardry he transformed the country, giving Wales breath taking, natural beauty beyond imaginings.

And after all his efforts and creations, the Dream Catcher summoned the elders to his home, in the dark depths of deep, deep underground to claim his reward.

Dragons Gold

Follow the daring adventures of two super heroes who take on the infamous Von Cach family.

With the future of the local mine and village at stake, Will and Dai stumble upon super powers and set about righting the wrongs of the evil Cach's.

The Infamous adventures of Wally Wainwright

Is he misunderstood? Is he really that bad? Is he to be believed? Read about his infamous journey and beyond. Read of how Wally evades death from the Silver Reaper, reunites a barnacle with his long lost family and make friends with a very cool seagull and rock legend

A funny and fascinating story to be enjoyed by children from the age of 8 to 11 years.

Snotty snoring seeps through a soft salty sand bed. Some wiggling and jiggling is followed by a very long and tired stretch. A sleepy eye opens, then slowly closes. This weary young worm isn't ready to wake.

Printed in Great Britain
by Amazon